...ket Street looking up towards
...897 (top) and below the same scene

...rs who can remember those days of
...back with fond memories.
...provides an important record of social
... will capture the imagination of
...ation. A few years from now, there'll
be no-one alive who can remember the days of
charabanc picnics, gaslit cobbled streets, steam
trains, rag and bone men, the old-style trams, clogs
and shawls. Yet the Mancunians of 2050 will be
able to reach for this book and know what life was
like in "the good old days." Then – and now.

David Thomas
Syndication Editor
Manchester Evening News

photos have barely changed. In others, the
landscape has gone forever, often replaced by
modern buildings and fast roads. The Manchester
Evening News, Britain's leading regional paper, has
teamed up with the city's Central Library to
produce this landmark volume. The unforgettable
photos of yesteryear are the pick of the bunch
from a huge collection kept by the library. They
have no less than 77,000 images stored on
computer which are easily accessible by the public.

But now you've the chance to cherish and keep
them for yourself along with an up-to-date record
of the hub of the North West as it is today. Based
on the MEN's weekly series "Then and Now" it
comprises not only photos but includes fascinating
stories to accompany the images, compiled over
the past two years by the newspaper's reporting
team. This book will be a favourite amongst more

D0544163

late 1800s

Upmarket move for old market

This 19th century view of bustling Chapel Street, Salford, is so dominated by the place known to everyone as the Flat Iron market, it hides the historical riches of the church sneaking into the picture on the left.

The Benefice and Parish of Sacred Trinity, Salford in the Diocese of Manchester – the full name given to it 1974 – is the only church so-named in the British Isles. Sadly, shortly after receiving the Communion for the first time in his new chapel, founder Humphrey Booth died on 23rd July 1635, and was buried in the Collegiate Church. The Chapel Street railway corridor, arguably a shadow of its former glory, passes the route of the former Flat Iron

market, which used to be in the grounds of Salford's oldest church.

Gone are the days when the market, which takes its name from its shape, was the place you could buy anything you wanted – from a rusty old cavalry sword, or a pair of skates, to a bunch of curtain rings, or a pair of half-Wellington boots.

Today, Chapel Street has no market but is enjoying an economic and social renaissance with people moving back into the once busy area. In 1998 it was included in a project to commemorate historic buildings and streets in Greater Manchester when it scooped £150,000 from the English Heritage and Heritage Lottery Fund partnership.

The growth of Manchester city centre is expected to spill into Chapel Street and Salford's city fathers are already making preparations to be part of the expansion with the building nearby of the five-star Lowry hotel and a number of penthouse flats.

Still a green refuge worth retreating to

It looks like a sleepy little backwater – and the three or four horse-drawn carriages captured in our 1895 snapshot of Wilmslow Road, Didsbury, give no hint that this was to become one of the busiest routes in and out of Manchester.

Even in those days, Didsbury was an attractive place to live for business and professional people working in the city. Today, the car is king of the road, but with nose-to-tail traffic on this artery to an area of commuter-land more popular than ever, it's hardly possible to travel much faster now than it was way back then, in that more leisurely age.

Apart from the cars, a time-traveller dropping into the 21st century from those last years of

the 19th would find the scene not unfamiliar, with most of the building fronts easy to recognise. True, the gables have gone from the building with the blind, which is now O'Neills, but the Victorian watering-hole – purveyors of Groves and Whitnall's Ales and Stouts – is still quenching local thirsts, transformed into the Dog and Partridge.

In the modern-day view, a bit more greenery and a clock-tower have sprouted to the left of O'Neills, in place of the old Didsbury railway station, which is now demolished.

Shops that survived the Blitz — and the Arndale

The stark yellow tiling of the Arndale is one of the most distinctive features of the modernisation of Manchester's city centre.

But sandwiched between the shiny ceramics of the retail palace and the glitz of the newly-opened Printworks entertainment complex, are a few treasures that have survived redevelopment —

and Nazi bombs.

On the left hand side of the street, Withy Grove Stores Ltd still occupies the building with the arch windows, as it has since 1850. The horse-drawn carriages are long gone but the safe specialists and office furnishers is still thriving.

Crossing Dantzic Street, the next shop up on the left hand side is the present site of T Stensby and Co Ltd – Gun and Rifle Makers. Although the shop

was then sited on the other side of the road out of view, the building has remained unchanged and still features a quirky gargoyle on its corner above the doorway.

Moving further up the street on the same side were a row of small jewellers shops. Today, there are still jewellers and second hand book shops on this stretch. On the left of the Withy Grove Stores at 33 Withy Grove was a saddlery and leather shop and at 31, on the left of the picture, was Marsh's store which sold household goods and specialised in fireworks.

The sign above the shop bears an advert for Payne's Fireworks – the famous Manchester manufacturer. These pictures reveal the impact that the massive Arndale shopping centre and its car parks have had on the area. The 1895 photograph was taken from the corner of Sugar Lane, a road that the development engulfed.

Scores of shops, a flea market, a flour warehouse, a street and a couple of pubs have made way for the mall. The area was nicknamed the Rovers Return market place after the original Rovers Return pub which was on the right hand side of the street behind the flea market stalls.

The stalls were mostly booksellers and the Warehouse behind them was owned by Boddington and Leigh. In the background, a three storey building can be seen in the older picture, the current site of the single storey Central Radio Ltd electrical goods store.

The top two floors were lost to a German bomb in the Second World War.

Quiet corner in a world of change

It was known as Poet's Corner in the late 1800s and you can certainly wax lyrical about these images.

Once a narrow, cobbled street lined with half-timbered buildings, Long Millgate, near Victoria Station is now an eye-catching open space, where the stunning Cathedral Gardens are surrounded by some of the city's most historic buildings.

In the 1895 image, the Sun Inn pub on the right was a popular stopping-off point for shoppers in need of refreshments. At the forefront, the Brown and Co fire appliance store window displays

all the equipment that householders needed.

The area was transformed after the IRA bomb in 1996. The current mix of historic and modern buildings combine to make this a renowned corner of Manchester. Karl Marx and Fredrick Engels were regular visitors to this area when they lived in Manchester and would have used the nearby free library, funded by Humphery Chetham, as they worked on the "Communist Manifesto".

The historic Chetham School of Music, originally founded as Bluecoat orphanage in 1653, is still there. Nearby, on the Victoria Station approach, the glazed canopy along the street frontage still displays the names of destinations. And overlooking the entire scene is the striking 400ft CIS Tower, one of the most distinguished in the city.

Putting life back into the historic heart of the city

Piccadilly Gardens in 1890 was full of the hustle and bustle of life in a thriving city.

Some things have not changed completely though, because on the left of the old photograph – taken from the top of Market Street looking towards Portland Street – are horse-drawn passenger trams, pre-dating today's Metrolink. To the right is the Manchester Infirmary, demolished in 1910 after the hospital was rebuilt in Oxford Road. The statue of Sir Robert Peel still stands on the corner of the gardens.

Today the area remains just as busy and the modern tram rails can clearly be seen. But in recent years Piccadilly Gardens have become run down. Now plans have been revealed for a sparkling new look which will see the gardens transformed into a European-style plaza with fountains, water jets and dramatic lighting.

The area will be overlooked by a five-storey glass-fronted building housing offices and restaurants and acting as a gateway to the city.

Pillars of the community columns mark a rich heritage

These grand images of Manchester's commercial heritage are a century apart – but there's something strangely familiar about the impressive columns gracing Heaton Park. They belonged to what was the old Town Hall.

But in the city's Victorian heyday mushrooming wealth and aspirations demanded a bigger and grander civic powerhouse – so a new town hall was built in Albert Square.

The original building became the Central Library, before that in turn moved to St Peter's Square as it continued to expand. But the neo-classical columns did not become part of the library when it moved, and when the original building was replaced the facade was

moved to Heaton Park.

Today, this stretch of King Street looks very different and is a centre for shopping. It boasts some of the city's poshest stores, with designer names like Hermes and Mulberry, and has long-standing links with the banking sector. Other parts of King Street have retained their Victorian style, with shoppers attracted by the tree-lined Dickensian charm.

Located on the south side of King Street, with Cross Street in the background, the throng of nearby retail outlets prove that the `old world' shopping centre in King Street is as popular as ever. The hustle and bustle looks the same in both pictures.

The clue to 21st century modernity are the cars lining the spacious streets. Horse-drawn carriages and old fashioned lamp posts are two of the more obvious signs of the difference a century makes.

King Street is regarded as one of the most exciting retail pitches in the UK. Traders and shoppers were quick to label it the Bond Street of the north.

Competition for a place in the area for the fashion elite has always been fierce, with names like Armani and Calvin Klein vying for attention – and all add their own glamour.

Museum's own little place in history

Hansom cabs may no longer wait outside but after more than 180 years, the road to culture still leads to Manchester Museum.

Famous to scholars all over the world, the scientific showcase was founded in 1868, yet its origins go back to 1821, when the Manchester Society of Natural History was founded.

Previously, Manchester Museum had occupied a site in Peter Street but today it is an integral part of Manchester University, in Oxford Road.

Financed and administered by the University of Manchester, the museum is renowned for having more than nine million specimens in its collections, including Egyptology and natural history. It also has an aquarium and vivarium – where living animals can be studied.

The collections are made as widely available as possible to scholars and the general public. From its early days the museum has run an education service. And it is hardly surprising that many of the 200,000 plus who visit the attraction each year are school children.

Boasting the best Egyptology collection outside London, the museum's 21 mummies, dating back to the first millennium BC, have yielded up secrets of the every day curses of life in ancient Egypt. These include chronic lung disease from inhaling sand, burrowing worms under the skin, smallpox and bad breath. The mummies are lavishly displayed along with X-ray pictures of their missing teeth and dislodged bones.

Another human relic which has brought crowds in is Lindow Man – the 2,000-year-old body preserved in peat which attracts up to 2,000 visitors a day. Two of the museum's other big draws go by the name of iguanodon and massospondylus – Manchester's own dinosaurs.

Horse sense rules

Horse drawn carriages were the norm when this photograph was taken in 1891. The picture is Stevenson Square looking towards Newton Street and Piccadilly.

The photographer has captured the square in a relatively-quiet moment compared to the normal hustle and bustle of life you would expect in the city.

Fifty years earlier the scene was not so peaceful as history books reported "a battle took place in Stevenson's Square between the Anti-Corn Law Leaguers and the Chartists, and several heads were broken." The square also witnessed demonstrations by unemployed men during the

General Strike in 1926. It also served as a terminal for electric trolley buses for many years bringing in hundreds passengers every day from Ashton, Stalybridge, Droylsden and Openshaw. Today's photograph shows that cars and vans are now the means of transport in the city centre.

However, the area still retains much of the character of the "old" Manchester, with its 19th century commercial buildings and warehouses. It had become the forgotten part of the city centre but a revival has been taking place in recent years. The square forms part of the Northern Quarter.

Grandeur that is Central Library

One is the picture of a fading Victorian age... the other an abiding monument to Manchester. The cobbled streets and bowler-hatted gentlemen of 1897 may have disappeared, but time has failed to dim the importance of Central Library.

Since it opened in 1934, the library has been a focus of municipal activity and stands as an impressive entrance to the city. Housed next door to the town hall extension, the library loses none of its grandeur.

The massive town hall facing Albert Square may be one of the city's most notable Victorian buildings, but looking up Mount Street, the partial image of Central Library jutting out on the right only tells part of the story.

Walk round the other side of the circular building and the distinctive style can be seen in its full glory. The entrance's unmistakeable five-bay portico Corinthian columns make the building instantly recognisable.

Nearby, another notable building is the Free Trade Hall in Peter Street, where Manchester's famous Halle Orchestra gave its first concert. It was well into the 20th century, however, before the city was able to build a Central Library fit for its great collections of books, periodicals and other materials.

Prime Minister Ramsay MacDonald laid the foundation stone in 1930 and it was opened by King George V in July, 1934. It was then the country's largest public library and remains one of the busiest, visited by more than one million people a year.

Good times, bad times

It is the city's focal point and the place where Mancunians have traditionally congregated to mark major events. With the town hall looming behind, Albert Square has seen Royal visits, New Year's Eve parties, football homecomings, street festivals and demonstrations.

The square in the 1894 image, is covered in decorations for a flying visit from Queen Victoria. She stopped off in the city on the way to open the Manchester Ship Canal and huge crowd gathered to welcome her. The Albert memorial, which was unveiled in 1867, can clearly be seen dominating the square. It was built in memory of Queen Victoria's Consort who died in 1861 and it was paid for by public donations.

At the time it was constructed, the surrounding land was undeveloped – the magnificent town hall was not built until 1877. In the mid 1970s, an appeal was launched to restore the memorial to its former glory and again the public dug deep.

Today, restaurants and offices line the square and traffic winds round the town hall. During the summer, hundreds of people enjoy lunch on the benches in the square and every New Year's Eve, a large crowd gathers to celebrate.

Faces of Jekyll and Hyde Road

There is plenty for historical detectives to get their teeth into in the picture of Hyde Road at Belle Vue, Manchester, taken in 1890.

Why, for instance, does the notice above the doorway behind the horse and carriage say Ashbury's Station, when the modern halt of the same name is a mile away in Pottery Lane?

One of the north west's first multi-screen cinemas, the Showcase, now stands on the site, and the whole area is steeped in Manchester's history. It will probably be best remembered for one of Britain's biggest zoos, which closed in 1977 after 140 years because of rising prices and the prospect of having to find thousands of pounds to replace much of the accommodation. But there were also fairgrounds, a ballroom, exhibition halls, restaurants and circuses. Now, the famous Belle Vue Speedway stadium is a car auction mart.

Stuart Bamforth, the former Belle Vue Speedway promoter and 1976 world stock car champion, died recently after a long illness. He bought the famous Hyde Road Speedway stadium and the team from Trust House Forte in 1982. They won the British League title that season and took the League Cup and Premiership titles under him the following year. He sold the stadium to British Car Auctions in 1987. Ashbury's station was opened in July, 1855, by the Manchester, Sheffield and Lincolnshire Railway (MS&L), a company that already had a comprehensive network of routes from Liverpool in the west to the east coast resorts. It was renamed Ashbury's for Openshaw just four months later and given yet another name, Ashbury's for Belle Vue, in August of the following year.

The MS&L directors, already responsible for the Woodhead Tunnel, went on to build a line to London. With the start of the works, the MS&L changed its name to the the Great Central Railway. Passenger services began from London on March 15, 1899. The building could be the present Belle Vue station in Hyde Road, on the line to Reddish and Marple, opened in 1875.

Don't go changing

It is one of the Manchester's classiest shopping areas, where even the McDonalds has been specially designed to maintain the upmarket feel of the place.

St Ann's Square is steeped in history and has changed little over the centuries. The old photograph of the square was taken in 1878 when the main menace to pedestrians would have been horse-drawn carriages rather than cars.

The history of St Ann's Square dates back to 1227 when Henry III granted Robert Greslet, lord of the Manor of Manchester, the right to hold a fair on St Matthew's Day. In 1708 Parliament gave permission for the building of a church on the site and a square was provided for the continuation of the fair.

The area was renamed St Ann's Square as a tribute to the reigning

monarch Queen Ann and Lady Ann Bland, patron of the church. She had the church built as a protest against the High Church teaching of the city's cathedral.

Bonnie Prince Charlie was cheered when he rode past in 1745. The church was completed and consecrated in 1712 and is the second oldest in Manchester. It originally had a spire which was removed in Victorian times and its appearance has not changed since then.

Like many parts of the city it suffered when the IRA bomb exploded, causing thousands of pounds worth of damage but it has now been restored to its former glory. Manchester's first outdoor war memorial unveiled in 1908 in the square honoured the soldiers who died in the Boer War. The dead came chiefly from the Manchester Regiment although they also included some who had volunteered.

More modern day changes have seen the pedestrianisation of the square which has made it a safe haven for shoppers and the building of a £300,000 fountain. In 1994 a £1 million facelift for St Ann's Square caused consternation among conservationists who claimed the large stone "cannonballs" were out of character with the 18th century and Victorian buildings. Despite their protests, the new look won many accolades and it has been copied in other cities.

Century of little change

There is little change to the front of most buildings – but the amount of traffic using the main road through Manchester city centre is certainly different.

More than 100 years ago cyclists and pedestrians were able to stroll casually along Deansgate. But that has changed as cars sit bumper to bumper as commuters and shoppers flock into the city. At night Deansgate remains just as busy as people pour into the city to enjoy its restaurants and bars.

Deansgate around 1895 at its junction with John Dalton Street and Bridge Street, the building on the right of the photograph has since been replaced with a bank.

Historians say the origins of its name remain unclear. It may have a connection with the deanery of the village church near Parsonage Gardens or when the Danes seized Manchester in 870 AD.

By the 1840s, Deansgate was a prosperous road with shops and fine houses fronting it, but it was a different story behind the facade where visitors took their lives in their own hands with criminals lying in wait. When social writer Frederick Engels toured these streets he was warned to take a guide with him.

Bombed but unbowed

It took a direct hit during the Second War and was badly damaged by IRA bombers but Manchester's Anglican Cathedral still stands proudly over the city.

And it is due to enjoy a new lease of life as millions of pounds are being spent on transforming the area dominated by some of Manchester's most important historic buldings. These pictures were taken from Deansgate looking towards the cathedral and Cateaton Street. The trams and horse-drawn carriages in the 1880 picture have been replaced by mobile storage huts for the workmen helping to create a city park.

It was in 1421 that Henry V granted a licence to Thomas de la Ware, Lord of the Manor of Manchester, to found a collegiate church. The following year the rebuilding of the old church of St Mary started. The choir and aisle were built between 1422 and 1458 and the nave holds the distinction of being the widest of any church in England.

Over the years the cathedral has suffered its fair share of setbacks – Second World War air raids and the Manchester bomb. The Regimental Chapel suffered a direct hit in the 1940 blitz, damaging a huge stained-glass window.

But the future for the area looks bright with the unveiling of the £4.2m city park scheme which will see dozens of trees and sculpted lawns replacing concrete and brick and a planned new visitor centre for the cathedral.

1900-19

Changing face of St Peter's Square

Central Library has been one of Manchester's most distinctive landmarks for more than half a century.

Together with the town hall extension, it provides a familiar, imposing and much-admired backdrop to St Peter's Square. But for more than 100 years before the dawn of the 20th Century, Mancunians knew the location as the site of an equally striking, though completely different building – Wyatt's St Peter's Church, begun in 1788.

In 1905, when our view of St Peter's was taken from Oxford Street, the classical-style church

had only two more years left. It was demolished in 1907, although its outline remains in the middle of the modern square, in which the Cenotaph was erected following the Great War.

The then and now comparison reveals little remaining of the original scene, apart from Waterhouse's magnificent town hall clock tower in the background. St Peter's, originally designed with a spire, is gone, as are the buildings on both side of Oxford Street, including the old Prince's Theatre, replaced by modern structures.

The buildings behind St Peter's made way for the library, built in 1934 and the town hall extension, begun the following year.

Bustle is back on the street that refused to die

It was once one of Manchester's leading shopping thoroughfares and thousands flocked to its stores. Oldham Street formed part of the commercial heartland of the city centre.

This picture was taken in 1900 and shows the hustle and bustle of the area with people hurrying about their business avoiding the trams that were part of everyday life.

However, over the years Oldham Street fell into decline and became a notoriously run-down part of central Manchester. The opening of the Arndale Centre in the late 1970s exacerbated the downturn in the fortunes of the street. Stores moved away and "to let" signs soon became an all-too

familiar sight. However, in recent years there has been a turn around for the street which has always maintained its cultural diversity.

It has become home to alternative music and fashion stores like Afflecks Palace and the trendy Dry Bar. It is now at the heart of the Northern Quarter, the area between Piccadilly and Great Ancoats, and millions of pounds are being spent transforming this part of the city, creating new apartments and businesses.

However the cafes, chip shops and pubs of "old" Manchester still exist alongside their more trendy contemporaries.

Big & bold

History screams from these images of Market Street in Manchester's Piccadilly when the tradition was to do things in a big way.

For instance, one day in the late 19th century the crowds milling around this end of the city on occasions became so uncontrollable they overflowed into the road, snarled up the traffic and brought out the police reserves.

Scores of bright balloons had been released, each one dangling a large label which carried on one side in bold black letters the name Lewis's of Manchester; and on the other a list of bargains available in

the new store that had opened that morning in January 1880 – the third largest store in Europe with a staff of 3,000.

Some of the balloons were picked up as far away as Leicester; Rhyl and Ross-on-Wye, with reports that one had floated to a town in northern Italy.

When it opened it claimed the largest food hall in Manchester; and was the only store in England with its own exhibition hall – and the only store in Market Street with its own fish and chip bar.

Outside the Royal Hotel, where the Football League held its first meeting in April 1888, men in bowler hats reflect the Victorian fashion and give an illuminating insight into a true provincial city. Sadly, Manchester's oldest department store closed in February last year after 121 years of trading.

Today discount retailer Primark occupies the ground and first floors, with TK Maxx in the basement. Lewis's went into receivership in 1991 and was bought by Liverpool-based Owen Owen. Marks and Spencer moved into the basement after the IRA bomb while their new store was being built but left the premises in 1999.

At the city's heart

Although the different forms of transport seen in Manchester's Piccadilly in 1915 would look strange today, there is still something very familiar about the city's central area.

Three different types of transport rubbed alongside in the early part of the 20th century. First in line and partly obscured, is a trolley-bus, a double-decker run on electricity, through trolley poles. An environmental dream, it was quiet, fume-free and more flexible in traffic than a tram.

It could accelerate like a sports car and stop on a sixpence. Side by side, are two horse-drawn wagons and a driverless car, a tell-tale sign of the coming transport revolution. In the background of the picture taken with Oldham Street on the left, you can just make out the old BBC building among a smattering of offices boasting grand architecture. The white buildings on the right are still there as is nearby Clayton House, home of the Manchester Lancashire Family History Society.

Today, the thoroughfare once cluttered by traffic has more open spaces for pedestrians, but the shape of the surrounding area looks very much the same. After years of decline, regeneration has thrown up some eye catching residential and leisure conversions.

1900-19

A secret snapshot of history

These people going about their daily lives at the turn of the 20th century were unaware that their movements were being captured on film.

Photographer Samuel Coulthurst took the picture in Rochdale Road, Collyhurst, around 1900, near to the junction with Angel Street.

The liveliness of the scene contrasts with the present day. Coulthurst managed to capture the hustle and bustle of everyday life at the time.

People did not have motor cars, so it was a case of walking to the shops or using horse drawn transport. Rochdale Road was a hive of activity with people

milling about using the stores.

Today the sight of people walking to and from the shops along this stretch of road has been replaced with thousands of cars as commuters pass through the area everyday to get to work in the city centre.

A return ticket as trams come back

The laying of tram tracks proved a real showstopper back at the start of the 20th century.

This photograph was taken in 1901 and shows lines being laid at St Mary's Gate in the city centre. The view is looking towards Deansgate at its junction with Blackfriars Street.

At the time, the trams were an established part of Manchester life and remained so until 1949. Today's picture shows just how much the car dominates the city's streets. Thousands of vehicles pass through Deansgate every day and the traffic is often reduced to

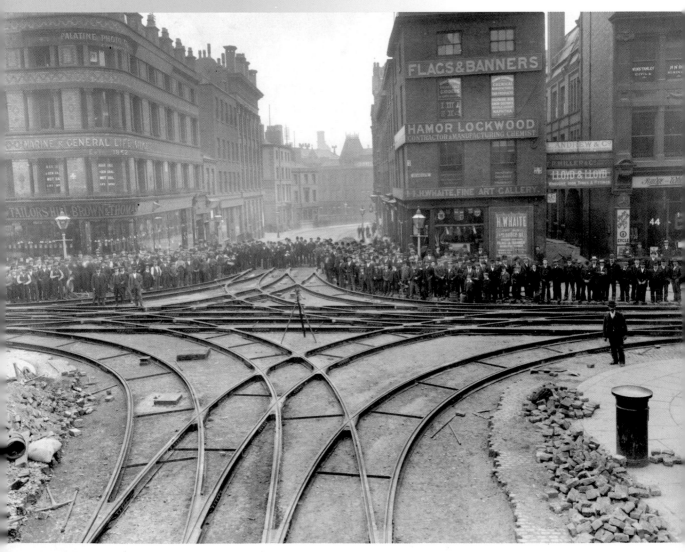

a crawl at busy times.

Even though the trams no longer run along Deansgate they have made a return to the city centre. When the last one left Hyde Road depot back in January 1949, people lined the city streets to watch. The No. 1007 travelled into Piccadilly then out along London Road before terminating at Birchfields Road depot.

Manchester was among the last of the local city and borough councils to sever its links with the trams. Diesel-engined buses and the spread of the motor car signalled the death of the trams.

How many of those who saw the tram make its last journey would have thought that they would once again become part of the city's life? But that is exactly what happened in the early 1990s when new trams were reintroduced. They proved so successful the service has been expanded.

All change as trams reach journey's end

It will be hard for many motorists to believe that Levenshulme was once a rural community.

There are records dating back to the 13th century but even by the 16th century there were only 25 people paying rates!

It was not until the middle of the 19th century that the population exploded with the industrial revolution but our picture of Stockport Road tram terminus in 1910 shows a very different scene from today's rush hour.

The view is towards Manchester city centre with Albert Road and

the Railway pub on the left.

Stockport Road is now one of the busiest in Greater Manchester. But the number 37 trams which once ran along the route to Stockport had no difficulties with traffic congestion. Manchester Corporation had gradually electrified its trams and there were more than 200 miles of tram tracks.

In 1930, Manchester became the first city to start replacing its trams with motor buses and all the trams had gone by 1949 – until Metrolink in 1992.

1900-19

All change for grimy station

The first view of Manchester for millions of visitors has long been Piccadilly rail station – and its grime. So it was welcome news when plans for a £55m refurbishment were announced in time for the Commonwealth Games.

The picture below shows Piccadilly Station in 1912, when it was called London Road and when direct rail travel to London was possible in nine and a half hours.

Its original iron sheds, with their decorative cast iron columns, were built in the 1880s and the 1842 Railway Crest still adorns the entrance, but most of the classic warehouses and goods stores were demolished in the mid-1960s refurbishment when the station also changed its name to Piccadilly.

In the recent years, more than £27m has been spent on new facilities, including the fixing of 10,000 individual panes of glass in the roof and a new major entrance directly off London Road.

Glorious revival for canalside

The glory days had long gone when this photograph was taken of the Bridgewater Canal in 1903.

The bleak scene in the centre of Sale shows a lonely boat tied up alongside a rubble strewn builder's yard, with the roof of Sale railway station just visible in the top left corner.

In its heyday, the Bridgewater Canal brought prosperity to Manchester by the barge load. It was built for Francis Duke of Bridgewater 240 years ago, to move coal from his mines at Worsley and was directly

responsible for the great surge of canal development during the Industrial Revolution.

Once it would have been the scene of constantly moving barge traffic but the coming of the railway age marked the start of a long slow decline. Today, however, the waterway is set to enjoy renewed prominence. Water traffic may be much quieter, and consists almost entirely of leisurely pleasure craft, but nevertheless the canal is becoming a focal part of the new-look centre of Sale. The stylish building on the second picture may look like a huge Victorian lock-keeper's cottage. In fact it is a pub built only five years ago. Innovative pub group Watling Street Inns bucked the modern trend when they created the King's Ransom, which features a Scottish type baronial hall with hunting trophies, stone archways and cosy sitting rooms.

Workhouse that nursed the Nightingale legacy

It was once home to those who had fallen on hard times or were suffering from ill health in Victorian Manchester.

The imposing Withington Workhouse provided basic shelter for men, women and children. The old photograph shows the chapel at the building in 1900.

The workhouse on Nell Lane was built in 1854 on 100 acres of open land which served as a home farm supplying cereals, vegetables and bacon for the workhouse kitchens and provided occupation for those who found themselves living in the building. Straw from the cereal crops was also used for

stuffing the workhouse beds.

By 1870 eminent architect Thomas Worthington had added five hospital blocks for the care of the sick and poor. They were designed on the advice of Florence Nightingale.

There were gardens where people suffering from mental illness could enjoy walks. Children had lessons in the three Rs and basic history and geography. Older boys were taught gardening, shoemaking, joinery and tailoring in workshops on the premises.

During World War I the military authorities took over the main building and when they relinquished it in 1920, it reverted solely to hospital use.

Nowadays the workhouse is long gone and in the place of the chapel stands the Nightingale Centre. It is the site of the Manchester Breast Screening Service, one of the largest breast screening units in the UK responsible for checking 140,000 women.

From horse to car

Traffic lights now stand near the spot once occupied by a blacksmith's forge. The passage of time from horsepower to the motor car could not be better illustrated.

The gap between these two images is a little more than 100 years and is a vivid guide to how much the landscape has changed. But this stretch of Middleton Road, outside one of the entrances to Heaton Park, only tells a part of the story.

The sight of a horse-drawn wagon in 1901 hints at a more tranquil time on the roads, and behind the trees that line the busy thoroughfare a 600-acre former country estate continues to hold a special place in the hearts of the generations that still enjoy visiting it. Bought by the city council in 1902, the park's boundaries on the Middleton Road side hide the rolling landscape and brilliant views across Heaton Park which could be seen during the 18th and 19th centuries.

Closer inspection takes you to the historic buildings nestled among the park's sprawling tree population. Grade 1 listed Heaton Hall, designed by architect James Wyatt for Sir Thomas Egerton in 1772, is acknowledged as one of the most important neo-classical stately houses in the country. Sadly, when Manchester town hall bought it in 1902 with surrounding Heaton Park, some of the precious contents were retained by the previous owner and the rest sold off in two auctions. It meant most of the original furnishings, some designed by Wyatt himself, were lost.

From cobbles to traffic jams

Taken in 1909 this picture shows Levenshulme station in Albert Road, looking towards Stockport Road, which today is a busy carriageway noted for its antiques and furniture shops.

The solitary man with a horse-drawn cart contrasts with today's image of cars waiting to pass under the bridge. One can only guess at what time of day the picture was taken, but Levenshulme was far from a quiet and lonely place. Like most other areas in the city, this south Manchester suburb was transformed during the years after the Industrial Revolution.

Levenshulme became home to many of the workers who toiled

in the local mills. During the late 19th and early 20th century, terraced homes were built to house the workers and their families and some of these properties still stand today.

The original arch of the railway, which can be seen in the earlier photograph, was replaced in 1950. Before the arch disappeared, only single-deck buses were allowed under the bridge.

1900-19

Enduring Splendour of Harley Street

The houses lining both sides of St John Street off Deansgate in Manchester are not just fine examples of Georgian architecture.

Today the once-genteel residential district where horses and carriages were seen daily is renowned for its specialist GP practices, private consultants, barristers' chambers, and other professions in the Grade II listed buildings.

It's an address affectionately known as 'The Harley Street of the North.' Flanked by Deansgate, Quay Street and Castlefield in the city centre, it is a recognised conservation area. Sadly, the

imposing church in the background was demolished in 1931. St John's church was built by Edward Byrom in 1767 as a memorial to his father John Byrom – writer, poet, diarist, inventor of shorthand, and Jacobite sympathiser.

A lovely building with a spire containing eight bells and a clock with four faces, St John's no longer exists and St John's Gardens now stands in its stead. Amazingly, most people pass without an upward glance at a blue plaque on a building at the corner of St John Street and Deansgate. It marks one of the most significant spots in Manchester's history.

If you had been standing there in September 1642 you would have had a grandstand view of the bloodiest of battles in the Siege of Manchester during the English Civil War.

City of dreams

It provided a source of recreation for thousands of Mancunians and people from all over the north west.

In its time White City on Chester Road, Old Trafford, served as an amusement park featuring a water chute, miniature railways and shows. It also staged athletics, soccer, rugby and stock-cars all in front of massive crowds.

And at its peak it was one of the best greyhound tracks in the country. About 100 dogs were on the racing strength and there were 60 bookmakers.

Over the years thousands of people flocked through the

stadium entrance to enjoy watching the varied sporting events, as seen on the photograph taken in 1900.

However the fortunes of the arena fell into decline during the 1970s and in 1981 the final greyhound meeting took place with several hundred punters braving the drizzling rain to enjoy one last bet.

The site soon became derelict and was eventually sold in 1988, bulldozed before being turned into a thriving shopping and leisure park.

City concert hall started musical trend

Two hundred years ago Manchester was as much a boom town as it is today. But in a city that has been happily recycling itself since Roman times, Lower Mosely Street could easily fill a glorious chapter of its own.

Back in 1830 there was the famous Gentleman's Concert Hall, standing imperiously on the site now occupied by the Midland Hotel.

Our picture showing the Bridgewater Hall and offices on the right and St Peter's Square in the background, illustrates the jigsaw of regeneration.

The great cotton warehouses have become stylish homes and offices, Central station is the G-Mex and the Bridgewater Hall

will be admired for generations.
   A hundred years ago, Lower
Mosley Street was a busy
thoroughfare of offices, shops and
restaurants, including Platts,
which specialised in tripe dinners.

City's art and soul

Trams were the main form of transport in Manchester at the turn of the 20th century.

Taken in 1905 this photograph shows a policeman standing in the middle of the road as the hustle and bustle of city centre life goes on around him. But few would have imagined that nearly 90 years later, the trams would reappear on Mosley Street.

The City Art Gallery on the corner of the junction with Princess Street recently underwent a multi-million pound renovation.

The building was designed by

Charles Barry, who was also responsible for the Houses of Parliament and constructed between 1827 and 1835. It was built to house the Royal Manchester Institution, which sought the "promotion of Literature, Science and the Arts."

However, dwindling funds led to the Manchester Corporation taking possession of the building in 1883 and running it as the City Art Gallery. Treasured works from the gallery, including the world-famous pre-Raphaelite collection and major works by Turner and Constable, have been on loan at galleries throughout the world.

Lost in the rush, a little oasis of peace in the city

It forms an oasis of greenery in the middle of industrial Manchester and most people would not know it existed.

Little may have changed in the image of Old Tan Yard in Gorton, taken in 1904, but the surrounding area and the pace of life are totally different today. The photograph, was taken from near the bottom of the hill down from Hyde Road with Gorton Brook running under the bridge.

In the early 20th century, Hyde Road was not the busy carriageway it is today as thousands of cars and lorries now travel along this route to and from

Manchester. Then, children could still play happily in the road without parents worrying about traffic. To the left of the old picture was Springbank Farm which today is now forms part of Springbank Farm Kennels and Cattery.

To the right of the picture, are a group of cottages that formed part of the tan yard workshops and also played home to the people who worked there. The workers produced leather for the hat factories in Denton. Some of older readers will also remember using Old Tan Yard as an improvised skating ring.

During icy wintry weather youngsters would use the hill to slide down. Just on the other side of Hyde Road a similarly picturesque scene is painted in Far Lane. It could be a leafy lane in Cheshire yet it is only yards from the juggernauts that thunder along the A57.

Little corner in the history of prosperity

The year is 1907 and at High Bank House, it was a case of at home with the wealthy Grimshaw's.

Once a symbol of the area's prosperity and permanence, High Bank in Gorton is now sadly missing. Today, the same spot that was home to a local landowner is occupied by a bowling green, partitioned off by a low brick wall and high railings.

Highbank House is situated on High Bank, the continuation of Tan Yard Brow. In 1841, it was the home of John and Elizabeth Grimshaw, presumably man and wife, and a George Grimshaw. By

1861, a new Grimshaw family were in residence: John and Mary Grimshaw and their three sons.

The eldest son, John, was a solicitor, Joseph was a barrister and their youngest son George was a cotton spinner. The Grimshaws of 1861 were still in residence in 1881, with the exception of Joseph and the father.

A little to the north of High Bank House and on the same side of the lane was High Bank Farm, owned by James Grimshaw, who farmed 15 acres. In 1881, it was occupied by James Brocklehurst and his wife, who then farmed 40 acres.

Although not shown in our images, it was common practice in the 19th century for mill owners to build or buy cottages for their workers.

Industrial mill town moves on

Nearly a century stands between these two images on the banks of the Rochdale Canal – but the future looks bright for the famously 'Satanic' mill area of Ancoats.

The concentration of so many cotton mills led to Ancoats being labelled the first industrial suburb in the world. It was here that the industrial revolution came of age, and the spinning mule and the steam engine came together for the first time.

During the 1930's a luxury yacht called the Marali navigated the full length of the canal on payment of £3 3s. 8d. in tolls. Occasional through traffic persisted until 6th April 1939.

On June 12, 1939, the final passage was completed by May Queen travelling light from Sowerby Bridge to Manchester on her way to being sold. On May 29, 1958, the last boat from Bloom Street Power Station passed down the canal through Manchester to the Bridgewater Canal and commercial traffic ceased.

At its peak, it was a thriving but dirty and polluted place, where poor housing for the workers was defined by the huge redbrick mills in which they worked. It is still home to Murray's Mill, in Redhill Street, which dates back to 1798. Not far away, the Ice Plant attracted an ice cream industry – and 2,000 Italians. For more than a century it was an economic powerhouse, but the area fell into steep decline along with its main employers – the cotton trade and manufacturing industry.

Today, restoration work is underway to clear the silted canal to make way for a vibrant living quarter.

From tramways to take-aways

Once they were grocers, watchmakers and milliners but now the shops on this busy south Manchester street are take-aways, estate agents and restaurants.

The growth of our fast food culture has graphically changed the face of the businesses plying their trade from the dominating Victorian facade of the Oak Bank Building on Wilmslow Road.

Back in 1912, the stretch of the street running between Davenport Avenue and Queen Street West in Withington was home to tailors, hairdressers, fruiterers and confectioners.

Now with the shops much more tuned to modern needs they

include Indian and Chinese take-aways, estate agents, an Italian restaurant and the Victoria Pub.

Out of shot is the distinctive-looking Withington Library which remains externally virtually unchanged and caters for readers and researchers six days a week.

Today, estate agents Bridgfords can be seen on the north side of Davenport Avenue where formerly there was parkland bounded by Rippingham Road and Moorfield Street.

The Victorian canopies of the Wilmslow Road side of the Oak Bank Building may have gone but the Wall to Wall carpet shop has provided a traditional feel to the buildings by re-introducing them over the Davenport Avenue pavement.

The original tall chimney stacks have lost some of their stature today as the rigours of wind and rain forced owners to partially demolish and re-seal the leaking brickwork.

The tramlines running from the centre of Manchester through Withington are unmistakable, as are the horse-powered trams. The first of these were introduced towards the end of the 19th century and by the 1930s Manchester trams were carrying more than 300 million passengers a year. The last of the old breed of tram made its final journey in 1949.

High-class square's selling point

Time has not withered the historic and architectural magnificence of Manchester's St Ann's Square, but it is a modern day attraction that holds the key to its enduring appeal – shopping.

With its select grouping of high class and expensive shops neatly tucked away, the city's most prestigious retail centre is as salubrious and popular as ever. An example of early fashion chic as seen in the picture taken around 1900 by Samuel Coulthurst – men in top hats with walking canes, women resplendent in long dress and bonnet – is better represented today by designer names such as Gucci, Versace, and Calvin Klein.

Appropriately, the horse drawn hansom cabs capture the hustle and bustle in St Ann's Square at the start of the 20th century in the same way that people and cars do now. In a recent study, Manchester was found to be the UK's second most popular location for retailers outside London – thus confirming the success of the area which encompasses King Street, St Ann's Square and the Victorian Barton Arcade. City centre shopping facilities have been targeted for environmental improvements, and the growth of complementary businesses, such as café bars, has further increased attractiveness for shoppers. As a result, smaller scale and specialist retail areas around the core are also flourishing. But it should be remembered that the St Ann's Square we see today didn't wait until the Victorian period to establish its commercial and retail roots. In 1708, when it was formed, city fathers ensured that St Ann's Square was made wide enough to accommodate the annual Acres Fair which had been granted to the people of Manchester as far back as 1301.

Hidden treasures of a city square

Few, if any, Mancunians are old enough to remember St Peter's Church in St Peter's Square. For its days were almost up when our picture was taken in 1907. It was demolished later in the same year after more than 100 years gracing the site.

Consecrated in 1794 – the same year as St Mary's Roman Catholic Chapel in Mulberry Street was built and John Dalton reported his discovery of 'Daltonism', or colour blindness, at a meeting of Manchester Literary and Philosophical Society – work on the construction had been begun by Wyatt six years earlier.

Its outline remains in the middle of the modern square, in which the Cenotaph was erected following the First World War. The building on the right of the picture, at the corner of Oxford Street, has now been replaced by unlovely modern buildings.

But, for once, the modern view actually outstrips the ancient one. The famous Central Library and town hall extension were not built until 1934. And the demolition of the church has also brought Waterhouse's magnificent town hall clock tower into view from Oxford Street.

In August 1819, a bloody crackdown by troops on people near St Peter's Church protesting about poor working and living conditions was christened "the Peterloo Massacre". Fifteen protesters were killed.

Green oasis set to thrive again

It's more like Blackpool on a busy day, as hordes of people young and old relax in the sunshine in the idyllic surrounds of Manchester's Heaton Park.

The Edwardian picnic scene from 1906 perfectly captures the essence of a bygone and more graceful era. The biggest municipal park in Britain, Heaton in its heyday was always a huge draw for Manchester families.

By contrast, in our up-to-date picture, a walker with his dog in the same spot cuts a solitary figure. But under a huge Lottery-funded scheme, Manchester council is already on its way to restoring the park to its

Edwardian glory.

More than £9m has been awarded by the Heritage Lottery Fund – the largest grant ever given for such a scheme. The ultimate aim is to transform it into a park to rival Cheshire's Tatton or Dunham Massey. Six centuries ago the rolling pastures of Heaton formed part of the great estates of the Langleys of Agecroft Hall.

The land passed by marriage to the Egerton family, later Earls of Wilton, and fell into public hands when it was bought by the Manchester Corporation for £230,000 in 1902. Generations of families have enjoyed the delights of Heaton Park on hot summer days, boating on the lake, strolling through the gardens, bowling, and playing golf.

The gem in the Heaton crown is Heaton Hall built in 1772 by Sir Thomas Egerton. The handsome Georgian mansion with its trademark lions, was designed by architect James Wyatt, and is acknowledged as one of the most important neo-classical stately houses in the country.

In recent years Heaton has played host to a variety of spectacular events, ranging from a visit by the Pope in 1982 when the park was the seventh most visited tourist attraction in the UK, to sporting, theatrical and musical occasions.

The park has twice been the pop broadcasting centre of the nation when Radio 1 went out live from Manchester.

Golden days of the vital link to docks

It's a long way from San Francisco but Trafford's swing bridge has been Manchester's golden gate for more than 100 years.

A testament to the great Victorian era in which it was built, the iron bridge in Trafford Road has linked Salford Docks at Ordsall and White City, Old Trafford, since the Manchester Ship Canal officially opened in 1894.

Back then it provided passage for a different type of traffic, including trams and horses and carts carrying goods to waiting ships. Soon the carts gave way to cars and now the bridge carries droves of Manchester United fans who flock to nearby Old Trafford to watch their footballing idols.

Thankfully, there are no longer infuriating hold-ups as the bridge opens – it was permanently opened to vehicles in 1992. Often there were agonising delays for hundreds of cars and lorries when the bridge let ships through at rush hour.

The gleaming trams have long since gone, but just a stone's throw away, the next generation Metrolink station stands proudly on the horizon. More recently historians were up in arms when two large wicker baskets, which had been an eye catching feature of the bridge, mysteriously disappeared following restoration work.

The "lobster pots" acted as traffic controls for the ships. When one basket was raised, crews would know which ship had right of way. The other acted as an early warning system, letting people know when the bridge was about to swing. In fact the baskets had been removed by the council for safe-keeping and were later returned.

Years wipe out an oasis of calm

Taking a well-earned break from his slog in the fields, a worker sits and contemplates the idyllic rural scene before him. Wearing a stylish hat and smoking a roll-up with his tools laid carefully beside him, he appears to have not a care in the world.

But were he able to sit on the wall in the second picture, our friend would most likely feel he had stepped into another world. It is exactly the same spot, but the fields are gone, there is a garage where the barn once stood and traffic zooms down the busy road in the heart of Levenshulme.

Both pictures show the junction of Wellington Road and Crossley Road – which was called High Lane at the time of the main photograph which dates from 1900.

Then it was a typical pastoral spot set in the midst of acres of farmland and rolling hills. Henry Ford may have built his prototype car four years before this picture was taken, but the advent of the automobile in Levenshulme was still years away and the only sound that could be heard – apart from the occasional clatter of a coach and horse – was the bleating of spring lambs.

But now it is a busy city suburb, on the main road between Manchester and Stockport. The hay bales and barn of Black Brook Farm are long gone, replaced instead by a McVitie's factory, the corner of which can just be seen on the right of the modern shot. Cars clog up the junction and the only animals to be seen or heard now are pet dogs.

Workers in 1900 were able to watch the world go slowly by. But what was true then is still true now – time waits for no man.

Why Hitler had his eye on the Rolls-Royce hotel

It is regarded as Manchester's finest hotel and some of the world's most famous people have stayed under its roof.

Winston Churchill, Frank Sinatra, Bing Crosby, Laurel and Hardy, Princess Anne, Pavarotti, John Major and more recently Mike Tyson have all made themselves at home in the luxurious surroundings of The Midland.

The Crowne Plaza Manchester – The Midland, to give it its full title, dominates the approach to the heart the city. The old picture was taken in 1910, seven years after it opened and shows the front of the hotel and St Peter's Square.

The building to the right is no longer there and is now the site of Manchester's Central Library.

The hotel was built by the Midland Railway Company near to Central Station and was designed to promote the firm's railway as well as its hotels. But one of the first meetings at the hotel has gone down in the history of the motor car. Charles Stewart Rolls and Frederick Henry Royce met at the hotel on May 4, 1904 and agreed to form the now world famous Rolls-Royce motor company.

During the Second World War military top brass and Winston Churchill stayed at the hotel. It was even reported that Adolf Hitler thought the building was so beautiful he gave orders for it not to be bombed during the war.

In fact, Hitler was so impressed with pictures of the hotel that he planned to make it his base after the Nazis had invaded Britain!

The hotel stands at the top of Peter Street which has recently become one of the most popular destinations for late night revellers but clearly it has lost none of its splendour.

Village gem's historic tale

Every picture, they say, tells a story – but not all as fascinating as the one behind this historical gem to be found in a south Manchester suburb.

Northenden owes much of its character to the fact that it was once an attractive riverside township for the city's more affluent managers, clerks and tradesmen.

In the wake of Manchester's acquisition of nearby Wythenshawe for a new "garden city", Northenden became an official district of Manchester in 1930. But the juxtaposition of this up-to-date photo and a snapshot from 1910 hides a little-known

fact about St Wilfrid's Church, which can be seen in the background of both pictures.

People have worshipped on the site from at least Saxon times and Norwordine, as it was then known, gets a mention in the Domesday Book of 1086. Back then, medieval salt merchants forded the nearby river Mersey.

Today, Church Road boasts an off-licence and a nursery school. The Church Inn, which is visible in both pictures, often hosted jazz sessions in the "trade boom" of the early 1960s.

Busy Church Road is a sign of how Northenden has felt many of the pressures of the 20th century, not least those resulting from a rapid increase in traffic.

Nearby Palatine Road has become a busy commuter route, while the building of the M63 and the extension of Princess Parkway to form the M56 have brought opportunities and pressures for Northenden. With easy access to the city, airport and national motorway network, opportunities for business development are considerable, although it could be argued that such a development sometimes struggles to be compatible with the existing fabric and amenity of the area.

HUDSON, Paul 22/9

Victorian market site set for huge facelift

It used to be one of the biggest markets in the country and played a vital role in Manchester life.

Today the hustle and bustle of Smithfield Market on Shudehill has been replaced by a more leisurely pace of life but plans are in place to revitalise the area.

The picture shows the market in 1907, as traders go about their business. The market was a vibrant place and helped put Manchester on the commercial map. It was built in 1853 and the fruit and vegatable market provided a covered trading area of more than six acres. It contained

around 500 stalls occupied by 130 traders and became the most important in the country apart from London's Covent Garden.

In 1872 the wholesale fish market was added to the site and this contained 70 stalls let to about 35 traders. But as the market grew, so did problems with the increase in traffic in the area, leading to traders and customers facing diffulties caused by congestion.

The market closed in 1973 and moved to a new site in Openshaw which could cope with large delivery trucks. The old market site is now due to enjoy a new lease of life with ambitious plans unveiled to revamp the whole area.

A monthly market has started and around £50m is due to be spent revitalising the Northern Quarter – and this will include new homes, businesses, shops and restaurants.

Up the junction

A corner of the city still bustling with life Portland Street at its junction with Princess Street was a hive of activity when this photograph was taken in 1905.

A policeman can be seen in the middle of the road maintaining order amid the hustle and bustle of early 20th century life. Horse drawn carts are being used to deliver items down a makeshift conveyor belt. Pedestrians share the road with a man on horseback and tram tracks can also been seen in the cobbles.

The side of the pub is plastered in adverts for items including Oxo, Nestle Food, Colman's Starch and Greenhalgh's Preserves, all

household names in their day. The famously tiny Circus Tavern with a 40-person capacity can be seen behind the man on the horse.

Today the buildings have hardly changed and the junction is still a busy thoroughfare. However pedestrians no longer have to worry about horses and carts, instead they have to avoid the hundreds of cars that pour through the junction every hour.

People can still enjoy a pint in the Circus Tavern and the Old Monkey which has replaced the Queen's Arms on the corner.

Theatre of dreams

During the 19th century, Oxford Street in Manchester developed into an important entertainment and shopping centre – but not without some controversy.

The Palace Theatre, or The Palace Theatre of Varieties as it was then called, opened on Monday, 18 May, 1891, with the grand ballet Cleopatra direct from the London Empire.

The decision to launch the theatre with such a cultured attraction was partly a sop to an organised body of church protest which had labelled the building a den of iniquity. Although the opening night was packed to the rafters, with a total capacity of

3,675 (including standing room), compared to today's 2,000, by 1894 the management had dropped the highbrow ballets in favour of giving the customers exactly what they wanted – variety, variety and more variety, from artistes including Charles Chaplin and music hall stars Vesta Tilley and Harry Lauder.

Ballet and opera returned on a regular basis in the 1950s, and the 1960s saw the advent of the London-bound musicals, not forgetting, of course, the ever-popular Christmas pantomimes.

The 1970s was a decade of decline and the threat of closure was imminent. But the future of the Palace was saved when the civil engineering and construction company Norwest Holst bought the theatre in 1978 and embarked on a three-year restoration programme.

Today, Oxford Street is humming with activity as a number of new developments take shape.

1900-19

Strong beat of city's medieval heart

Manchester's medieval heart, ignored by the Victorians, is once again emerging from its 19th Century commercial corral.

And in its centre, the cathedral and Chetham's school, which flank what was Fennel Street, are set to become key historic landmarks in a new verdant setting.

Here is the location of a new city park, one of the positive consequences of the rebuilding following 1996 IRA bomb, where strollers will soon appreciate Manchester's 500-year legacy in a pleasant, open and green setting, closeted no longer by decaying buildings and intrusive traffic.

Our archive picture shows the view across Fennel Street, taken from the cathedral side in 1900, with Chetham's mullioned stone frontage overshadowed by buildings, now largely demolished, dating from the mid to late 1800s.

The hansom cabs, drawn up on the cobbles, evoke the turn-of-the-century atmosphere. Chetham's Hospital and Library, as it then was, were described by Leland in 1538 as a "fair builded college" which was about 100 years old when he put quill to paper.

It is probably the oldest continuously inhabited place in Manchester, possibly dating back to Saxon times. The internationally renowned musical education institution was originally a baronial manor house, converted to a college, later dissolved with the monasteries in Tudor times and re-founded in 1651 thanks to the legacy of Manchester merchant Humphrey Chetham as a free public library and free school for 40 poor boys.

Specialising in music since the 1950s, the school now caters for almost 300 students, aged between eight and 18, selected by audition for their musical excellence.

Our present day view depicts a completely new vista with the school obscured by trees as the new park – the green open space central to the city's Millennium Quarter incorporating the under-construction Urbis Centre and a long-awaited cathedral visitor centre – takes shape.

Right royal drama

There has been many a drama behind the impressive facade of the Royal Exchange – but not all have been of a theatrical nature.

Before the impressive 192-year-old building was transformed into a theatre 25 years ago, it was the business centre of the city where traders would haggle and bargain over the sale of goods.

And with so many people gathered together, tempers at the Exchange could often reach boiling point. In 1812 troops had to be called when unemployed cotton workers broke in, smashing furniture, lamps and windows. And during the anti-corn law agitation 1842 exchange member John Bright was dragged away after mounting his seat to deliver a political speech.

As our picture – taken in 1905 – shows, the traders faced a steep climb up the stairs to the impressive Cross Street entrance to the Royal Exchange. But its distinctive facade had to be remodelled after being severely damaged in the Christmas blitz of 1940.

Across the road at the dawn of the 20th century were the offices of the Manchester Guardian and the Manchester Evening News, now based on Deansgate. And while both buildings in the foreground remain, as you peer further down Cross Street our pictures show the changes have been dramatic.

1900-19

On front page of history

The now-demolished Manchester Evening News and the Manchester Guardian Building made way for the Arndale Centre in the early 1970s.

The archive picture was taken in December 1902 by the city engineer's department. Then trams used to run up and down rails in between the cobbles of Cross Street. Built between 1879 and 1886, the site was bought for some £23,000 in four lots between 1860 and 1867.

As well as being home to the two papers, No. 3 Cross Street also housed Chubb's and Sons Lock and Safe Company, clearly visible on the south west corner

of the building on the corner of, what was then, Moult Street. Other occupants of the building included the Mercantile Bank of Lancashire and the Pahoria Cafe, next to Chubb's.

No. 1 Cross Street, visible in the background, was the office of the Manchester Courier newspaper which operated between 1825 and 1915. The building also housed the Ashton under Lyne Reporter.

Looking at the contemporary view of Cross Street, the MEN building would have stood half in Boots and stretched across the frontages of what is now the Abbey National and Halifax building socities.

Turn-of-the-century maps reveal the entrance to the then-collonaded Royal Exchange Theatre almost opposite that of the former Evening News and Guardian HQ.

The 30th anniversary of our move from Cross Street to Deansgate was celebrated recently.

1900-19

Not so very different

The picture taken in 1910 shows the junction of Rochdale Road and Old Lane, facing Boggart Hole Clough in Blackley.

Then, Rochdale Road was one of the key arteries into the city and it remains so today. But despite the continuity, there are a few surprises. The importance of the road was such that a century ago tram lines ran along it to the city centre.

Those lines are now long gone – much to the regret of the thousands of motorists who use the congested road. The period houses remain fairly unchanged, but sometime over the past 90

years a church has sprung up
behind them.

But perhaps most striking of all
are the people pictured. Then, a
man stood with his walking stick
and bowler hat, peering across the
road. Now, an Asian woman walks
along with her children, a
reminder of how Manchester has
become cosmopolitan.

Street motoring to bright future

The car had yet to become a familiar sight on Manchester's roads before the Second World War, but police were already making checks.

Whitworth Street, pictured here in 1930, at the London Road end with Piccadilly station to the right in the background. The two policemen have their backs to the old fire station which came to symbolise the city's defiance in the face of the German onslaught during the war.

The building was used as a police station and a coroner's court before the fire brigade left the site in the mid 1980s to move to its new premises in Thompson

Street. It is currently in mothballs having changed hands between various property developers. Just across the street is the former location of Pips nightclub, popular in the 1970s, and before that, the Twisted Wheel.

Today's image shows the building work, much of it developing apartments, which continues unabated in the city centre, and Monroes hotel can been seen on the corner.

Musical memories

Looking at these bland new apartments in the city, it is hard to imagine the architectural opulence that once dominated this stretch of Manchester's Oxford Street.

This particular location in our may stand opposite the Palace Theatre, but there is little evidence now of the city's key role as the north's financial centre.

For instance, between 1892 and 1912, commercial buildings such as the nearby Refuge Assurance offices (now the Palace Hotel) shone like beacons to the city's swelling wealth. Even banks outstripped those in London for display.

However, our view of Oxford Street in 1938 introduces Reno's,

a wholly different type of building and a musical era when big dance bands led the way. Then, owning a Lamy trumpet was the modern-day equivalent of having your first electric guitar.

As our picture shows, you could buy clarinets, saxophones, trumpets, trombones, snare drums and accordions on easy weekly terms. If today is all about boy bands, the thirties became a magical era for big band music, fronted by suavely presented crooners.

Reno's was one of the most famous music shops in Manchester and a magnet for teenagers who wanted to hear the latest sounds, or just stare adoringly at the shiny new instruments on display in the shop window.

The site on the corner of Whitworth Street West is now occupied by the apartments.

Market Street is in the clear

Rarely have two photographs so graphically shown the contrast between past and present as these pictures of Manchester city centre. Our archive photo was taken in 1934 and although you wouldn't know it, the location is the junction of Piccadilly Gardens and Market Street.

What is unbelievable in this day and age, is that while the scene looks as dark as night, it was actually taken in the middle of the day. Youngsters may have heard their parents or grandparents talk about "pea soupers" or smog, but thanks to clean air legislation they will never have experienced it. Scenes like this in the mid 1930s were a common occurrence in city

centres like Manchester, as the atmosphere became thick with the poisonous choking fumes of both home and factory chimneys. Smog – smoke and fog – brought city centres to a halt, disrupting traffic, but more dangerously causing dramatic rises in death rates.

As our photograph shows, the sky was so black the street lights were illuminated and cars and vans were running on full headlights. It is barely possible to make out the white-sleeved police officer on traffic duty at the junction, and the glow of shop lights in the background lends an eerie feel to the whole scene. What a difference from today's picture where the skies are clear, buildings are clean, and trees are growing in the pedestrianised square. During the industrial revolution, pollution often reached devastating levels with industries situated in towns and cities, and coal the sole source of domestic heat.

By the start of Queen Victoria's reign the dangers to health were fully recognised, but it wasn't until 100 years later that any real action was taken to limit smoke pollution. Manchester was a leader in pollution control initiatives. The National Smoke Abatement Society was formed with headquarters in Manchester in 1928, and in 1934 a secretary of the society first proposed the idea of "smokeless zones". The final turning point was the Great London Smog of December 1952. It lasted five days and caused an estimated 4,000 extra deaths. Manchester and Salford had the first smokeless zones in the country in the early 1950s.

Living the good life in suburbs

The leafy lanes of this south Manchester suburb have long been a fashionable area to live.

As seen in the image of Chorlton cum Hardy taken in 1935. A row of cars are lined up in the road as their well-to-do owners carry out their shopping in Wilbraham Road.

The motor vehicle was beginning to become a more frequent sight on the roads during this period, giving a taste of things to come. Old fashioned awnings outside the shops provided some shelter from the extremes of weather that

Manchester is subject to. During the 1950s and 60s the area became a magnet for famous sportsmen, celebrities and musicians.

Manchester United legend Sir Matt Busby bought a house in the area and lived there for almost all of his career and married life. Many of the Busby Babes rented property in Chorlton because it was close to Old Trafford.

Chorlton's other most famous residents were pop legends the Bee Gees who were raised in Keppel Road and went to school at nearby Oswald Road Primary.

Grand Old Lady reigns supreme

The Grand Old Lady of Oxford Street is as popular now as she was when the curtain rose for the first time on May 18, 1891 for a production of Cleopatra.

The Palace Theatre, was originally billed as the Palace Theatre of Varieties, and the first night was sold out to its original capacity of 3,675, compared to today's 1,996. It is hard to believe that this structure, once described by the local religious community as a den of iniquity, struggled to make any sort of profit with its early classic productions.

As a result, the programmes were quickly changed to cater for what the public wanted. While a

mixed programme of variety shows, musical comedy, and pantomime all followed, we would do well to remember the legendary actors, singers and dancers who have cut their teeth at the Palace.

The 1920s and 30s saw the likes of Alicia Markova, John Geilgud, Noel Coward, Gertrude Lawrence and Lawrence Olivier. And later it was British stars Tommy Steele and Marti Wilde who made the girls scream. Despite a sluggish period during the 1970s and 80s, the Palace still managed to establish itself as a premiere touring venue. The first ever production of Les Miserables played at the Palace to a sell out audience when the West End came to the north west. The theatre on the corner with Whitworth Street played host to Miss Saigon which proved to be another coup and box office smash for the Palace.

From eyesore to green oasis

Willow trees line the banks of the River Irwell to create a grassy oasis in an industrial landscape, but this part of Manchester used to be an eyesore.

Today's pretty view would have been unimaginable eighty years ago when the industrial revolution took its toll on the river's air and water quality, killing off marine and plant life. Albert Bridge was built in 1884 for the princely sum of £8,874, the bridge was used for hundreds of years by people travelling in horse-drawn carts and carriages.

The 1920 photograph, taken from the Salford side of the river, looks towards the Manchester side and features one of the River Irwell's landing stages for boats and barges. Maps and directories from the period list the occupations of people working in the buildings. Going on to the bridge is Albert Place, where there were dining rooms and a tobacconist's shop.

On Albert Street, which joined up to St Mary's Parsonage, there were electrical engineers and a printer in the building next to the bridge. There was also an antiques dealer, a portmanteau maker and the Standard Hotel. The hydraulic power station, which supplied electricity for a large area of Manchester, is now better known as the Pump House People's History Museum.

Lush vegetation, paths and quiet spots for fishing have replaced most of the industrial buildings. The transformation of the area is completed by multi-million pound property developments and a statue by sculptor Michael Lyons, the Doves of Peace, on Bridge Street.

Crossroads of change

They are figures frozen in time: a scene from a bygone era captured on film. The picture is all that remains as a reminder of a once-bustling road junction in Newton Heath, Manchester.

The setts and tram lines, not to mention the terraced rows of houses, shops and banks were long ago swept away. And the characters pictured – the local beat bobby included – stare towards the camera like silent ghosts of a vanished age.

Our photo of the junction of Dean Lane and Oldham Road, taken in 1924, bears no resemblance to the modern-day scene of a busy traffic junction. No trace is left of the shop signs,

Victorian gas lamps and a trader's barrow. Parr's Bank, in the centre of the picture, was as well known in its day as the NatWest is now. It was established in 1788. There were some 400 branches when it was swallowed by the Westminster Bank.

In 1920s Manchester, with thousands travelling on the third largest tram system in the country. It opened in June, 1901. Services reached Newton Heath by 1903, and by the end of the '20s there were almost 1,000 trams operating on 163 miles of lines in the city. But the tram was soon to fall victim to the advent of the bus. The city council took the decision to abandon trams completely in 1937, though the Second World War meant the axe did not ultimately fall until 1949.

Between the lines

In 1924, when the main photograph was taken, the power lines and tracks which carried trams to and from the city centre ran along Stockport Road in Longsight.

Today the road is one of the busiest in Manchester but the number 37 trams, which once ran along the route to Stockport had no difficulties with traffic congestion.

Manchester Corporation had gradually electrified its trams and there were more than 200 miles of tram tracks. Then in 1930, Manchester became the first city to start replacing its trams with motor buses. All the trams had gone by 1949 and none were seen

here until Metrolink in 1992.

But the same scene today shows just how much people have come to rely on their cars. The junction with Slade Lane is busy throughout the day.

In the old photograph a large billboard can be seen advertising a night out at the Ardwick Empire, which opened in 1904 and later became the New Manchester Hippodrome. There are still plenty of stores and pubs lining the route.

A gentler pace in suburbia

Road rage was unheard of in the 1920s and looking at this old photograph of Rusholme you can see why.

The sedate stretch of cobbled road and vintage cars is hardly recognisable as what has become one of the busiest routes into Manchester.

For modern motorists this junction of Wilmslow Road and Dickenson Road conjures up images of notorious traffic jams, but back in 1922 life ran at a much more leisurely pace. There were more pedestrians than cars, visitors to the city centre would ride in style on the number 821 tram and policemen escorted people across the road.

Trees lined the way of this affluent former agricultural area which had become Manchester's first suburb. The grand and rather impressive building at the junction is the Birch Villa Hotel, now transformed into the bustling Hardy's Well pub.

It was named after the Birch family who were major landowners in the area in the 1800s.

They later sold much of their land to another wealthy landowner Mr Dickenson – namesake of the road on which the hotel stands. The modern pub is recognised throughout the area for the Lemn Sissay poem written on the outside wall.

Changing face of students' haunt

This stretch of road will be well known to Manchester students both past and present.

These views of Oxford Road at the junction with Ackers Street on the left were taken 72 years apart. However, the only feature that remains is the spire of Manchester Royal Infirmary in the distance. Just visible on the left of the picture taken in 1930 are the gates of The Holy Name Church. The old photograph of the junction of Oxford Road and Ackers Street, bears no resemblance to the modern day picture of the city's bustling student area.

No trace remains of the overhead tram cables, shops or rows of terrace houses. Thousands used to travel on one of the largest tram systems in the country, with more than 1,000 trams operating on 163 miles of lines criss-crossing the city. The same scene today shows how much people have come to rely on their car, with Oxford Road one of the most congested in the city.

And pedestrians have to take care with a stream of buses heading for Fallowfield and Didsbury.

Hands of time move on

The massive clocktower on one of Manchester's most distinctive and historic buildings still watches over the hundreds of people who pour into the city every day.

But the trams that trundled along Oxford Road have now been replaced by cars and buses. In this image, the 217ft clocktower on the former Refuge building looms in the background.

People crossing the road had to keep a wary eye on the passing trams and the odd motorbike. Today pedestrians have to be avoid the hundreds of buses which leave the city via Oxford Road.

The former Refuge building was constructed in three phases, the

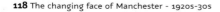

first part designed by Alfred Waterhouse in 1891, the second constructed by his son Paul with a final section added in the 1930s. The Grade II listed building was home to staff from the Refuge Assurance Company before they vacated the site in the late 1980s to move to Wilmslow.

It remained empty until a £4m refurbishment transformed it into the Palace Hotel in the 1990s.

Cobbles give way on road to the future

The overwhelming effect of the huge growth in popularity of the car is seldom more evident than in these two pictures of Ardwick.

The tramlines, cobbles and ornate facades are long gone from Ardwick's Downing Street, swept aside to make room for four lanes of tarmac and an elevated relief road.

The 1935 view of the street, looking north into the city centre, shows the old Co-op on the right hand side, a focal point for the local community, now replaced by warehouses and the southbound carriageway of the A6.

And on the left hand side of the

picture the junction of Grosvenor Street can still be seen but the well-known antique shops beyond it, although still present in the 1960s, were demolished to make way for the Mancunian Way.

The two-mile road was officially opened in May 1967 by the then Prime Minister Harold Wilson. One of few remaining buildings common to both views is the former Refuge Tower, visible on the skyline, now part of the Palace Hotel on Oxford Road.

The contemporary view is dominated by the multi-storey UMIST building on the left-hand side of the picture. An addition to the campus in the 1960s, the huge white tower is home to the maths and social sciences departments and is lit up at night. On the right hand side of the 2001 picture, the top storeys of BT's curved Victory House can be seen.

1940s-50s

Power to draw crowds

Daytrippers to Philips Park used to sit and wonder at this monument to Manchester's industrial power. Now they are flocking to the site for an entirely different reason – pedal power.

Once the most industrialised area of the city, the Bradford pit site has been totally transformed since this snap was taken in 1946. To the children seen here, playing in the sandpits, the looming Stuart Street Power Station was part of the landscape, churning out smoke and dropping grit onto the nearby houses.

A symbol of Manchester's immense productivity, the station was supplied with coal via underground tunnels from

neighbouring Bradford pit. First mined in 1740, the pit was once the deepest in England and many workers came from the immediate area. But by the early 1970s, there were increasing signs of subsidence and it was eventually demolished.

Now, with the construction of the Velodrome, the area has come to represent the new spirit of Manchester. The overbearing towers endlessly billowing smoke are long gone and in their place stands a symbol of the city's hopes for the future. The impressive £9m, 3,500-seat, aluminium-clad structure helped host the 2002 Commonwealth Games.

1940s-50s

A look at the great Britannia

The ranks of buses on Manchester's Portland Street are as familiar today as in 1955. The Britannia Hotel in the background remains one of the city's most distinguished buildings.

Portland Street, which runs along the east side of Piccadilly Gardens and continues to Oxford Street, was renowned for its 19th-century warehouses, and the Britannia (formerly Watts Warehouse), exemplifies Manchester's wealth and industry in the days of King Cotton. It opened in March 1858 as S and J Watts warehouses and offices, the city's largest building devoted to business, and each of its floors was given a different architectural

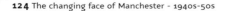

style. Inside, you will find Egyptian, Italian, 16th-century Dutch and Elizabethan styles, with the fourth floor based on the Versailles Galerie de Glaces.

As a warehouse, it summed up confidence and brashness, and inside the Britannia today, the original sumptuous staircase is preserved. The warehouse cost £100,000, took two years to build, and had a roof covered almost entirely by plate glass, the first time this was used in Britain.

Charles Dickens called it "the merchant palace of Europe". The building was badly damaged in the Blitz during the Second World War. On March 1, 1982, the building opened as a 329-bedroom hotel after a £5,000 conversion which retained all the striking exterior. In the entrance stands a 6ft bronze statue of Christ which was found in the basement. The statue, described by some as weak and lacklustre, was a memorial to Watts' employees killed in war and

was known by staff as St Bonus, as it was paid for with their Christmas bonus.

1940S-50S

Streets ahead

The part of inner city Manchester shown here has undergone a dramatic transformation in recent years.

Hulme was a symbol of urban decay during the 1980s but has a much brighter future thanks to the millions of pounds spent on redevelopment.

Stretford Road in 1955, a time when the bicycle rivalled the car as a popular mode of transport for the man in the street. A bike shop can be seen on the left of the photograph but today that has gone to be replaced by a symbol of the modern Hulme. The £4m Zion Centre is now on the road

which acts as a main corridor into Manchester city centre. The centre is aimed at 14 to 25 year olds and offers everything from dance and fashion, to rock music and the internet.

Hundreds of new homes have been built in the area to replace the notorious Crescents which had a nightmare reputation. The regeneration efforts have drawn widespread praise including words of support from the Prime Minister Tony Blair.

The glory that was All Saints

This festive scene shows people braving a snowstorm to go about their daily business. The picture, showing Cavendish Street by All Saints at the Manchester Metropolitan University just off Oxford Road, was taken in 1958.

The street used to continue along into Stretford Road and was lined with shops. One of the most important was Paulden's, which burned down in a famous fire the previous year causing £2m damage.

Newspaper reports talked of flames lighting up the All Saints area as the building was completely destroyed. The impressive building to the left of the photograph is the former Chorlton-upon-Medlock town hall which was built in 1830.

It was designed by Richard Lane, who was also responsible for the infirmary at Manchester Piccadilly and Salford town hall. In October, 1945, it was the meeting place of the fifth Pan-African Congress, an important event in the development of African nationalism.

Nowadays the building forms part of the main campus at Metropolitan University. The 170ft spire to the left of the image above belonged to the Cavendish Congregational Chapel, which was demolished in 1973. To the right of the photograph is Grosvenor Square, re-landscaped in 1995 as part of a transformation of the former polytechnic. During the last five years the university has undergone a major expansion programme, developing new buildings and refurbishment.

It now boasts more than 30,000 students and the area is a vibrant place during the day and night.

When the word on the street was American

The year was 1959 and in contrast to the staid corporate image it has today, one part of Manchester's Peter Street owed more to the growing influence of American life and its brash sensibilities.

Amid the quasi-Edwardian setting of the Cafe Royal – a magnet for the day's sherry and Black Forest gateau brigade – are the clear signs that all things American were making their mark on the city.

A giant poster advertising US film star Rod Steiger in the role of notorious Chicago mobster Al Capone screams out from the top of shop premises. And even the confectioners next door has the transatlantic spelling Kandy Box.

The Cafe Royal was bought by Mecca in 1944 and became a popular ballroom venue. Car enthusiasts will recognise the Nash parked outside the Kandy Box, a two-door hard-top convertible introduced in the US and Canada in 1954 and later built in England by Austin.

In the background and standing imperious, the circular Central Library is clearly visible. Only last year it underwent an extensive external cleaning programme and is now illuminated at night. The foundation stone of the library was laid by Prime Minister Ramsay MacDonald. Four years later on July 17 1934, King George V opened the building on a day so hot that many people in the crowd fainted.

Just before the library at the end of Peter Street is The Gaiety Theatre – ironically 1959 was the year it was pulled down – where you were thrown into the heart of Manchester's theatreland.

The Gaiety, bought by Annie Elizabeth Horniman with money left by her businessman grandfather, was Britain's first modern repertory theatre. Miss Horniman, who wore a monocle and sported a cigar for galas, produced more than 200 plays, and provided the English stage with some of its greatest actors.

By 1900, Peter Street and its environs was home to 20 theatres. Miss Horniman struggled to keep the Gaiety going until 1921, vainly seeking support from Manchester. Finally, she sold out to a Mr Abe Hollande for £52,500. She was made a Companion of Honour in 1932. She died aged 77.

Hospital built on a poor past

More than 40 years of city dwelling are revealed in these two images but they also conceal a little known fact about this thriving corner of Crumpsall in north Manchester.

Today, the junction of Crescent Road with Cheetham Hill Road looks as busy and prosperous as it did in 1959 but further along Crescent Road hides a feature that some of its past residents were less inclined to boast about – the workhouse. The institution which provided employment for paupers and sustenance for the sick, is on the spot where the North Manchester General Hospital now stands. But for many years 123 Crescent Road became a

euphemism for the workhouse.

The address would even appear on death certificates to avoid associated disgrace. In 1915, the Poor Law Unions in the Manchester area underwent a major re-organisation and as part of this change, the site was renamed Crescent Road Institution. With the official abolition of workhouses in 1930, the Manchester workhouse came under the management of the Manchester Public Assistance Committee, while the infirmary came under the hospitals sub-committee of Public Assistance Committee.

Later, as Crumpsall Institute, the former workhouse, which had always had its share of disturbed inmates, started to become a centre for treatment of the mentally ill. Crumpsall Institute was renamed Park House in 1939, and with the introduction of the National Health Services in 1948, became Springfield Hospital before changing its name again to Crumpsall Infirmary.

A quirky cricket history that doesn't need spin

Lancashire County Cricket Club was formed in 1864, but all the silver trophies, scrapbooks, caps, and other sporting paraphernalia you find crammed into oak-panelled cabinets only hint at the club's fascinating history.

Items associated with W. G. Grace, the most famous of early English cricketers, can be found in the club's museum, and the names of other famous cricketers remind you of the many colourful characters who, in their time, brought entertainment and glory in equal measure to the Old Trafford ground.

Formed as Manchester Cricket Club at the beginning of the 1880s, the club moved to the present Old Trafford in 1857. In 1865 when Lancs played their

first county match at Old Trafford against Middlesex the home side won by 62 runs. But the remarkable feature of the match involved the Middlesex under-arm bowler Vyell Walker who took all 10 Lancashire second innings wickets. In 1924 a Roses match ended in ignominy for the arch enemy Yorkshire. Needing only 57 to win they were bowled out for 33 by Cec Parkin and Dick Tyldesley.

The years 1963 and 1964 saw the emergence of a new name at Old Trafford, Cedric Rhoades. He launched the campaign which led to the historic meeting in Houldsworth Hall on September 24, 1964, when the motion "This meeting is dissatisfied with the conduct of the cricketing affairs of the club" was passed by 656 to 48.

In the 70s Lancashire became synonymous with entertainment, bringing excitement to the one-day game and attracting big crowds again. As the trendsetters of cricket they were John Player champions in 1969 and 1970, and Gillette Cup winners in 1970 and 1971.

Jack Bond, the then captain, had the help of two foreign stars in Clive Lloyd and Farokh Engineer – two overseas players who slotted in perfectly for the one-day cricket competitions.

Today, the Talbot Road end of the cricket ground boasts the Old Trafford Lodge, a superb new 68-bedroom development. With 36 executive rooms overlooking the famous Old Trafford pitch, you can watch county cricket from your bedroom window.

Animal attractions

It used to be Manchester's pet shop paradise, and many will have fond childhood memories of gawping at tortoises, cages of twittering budgies, and aquariums full of exotic fish in the city's Tib Street.

Our archive photograph shows the bustling and rather untidy street scene in 1959. The clutter and jumble of the nostalgic picture evokes a perhaps more innocent era.

Solid and comfortable old cars, rank alongside a plethora of hoardings and street signs, against a backdrop of the spire of St Paul's Church.

The disappearance of the former church leaves an obvious gap in the skyline of our modern day

photo; yellow lines ensure the highway is free of parked cars, and there is not an empty crisp packet in sight. The distinctive cake-style building in the background, now the Habib Allied International Bank, gives a sense of continuity to the scene.

Tib Street now boasts just one pet shop, Walter Smith's, but there is still a touch of the bohemian, with record and book stores, alongside cafes, jewellers, army surplus, and even sex shops.

The area, which has its origins in the 1780s, is now at the heart of the city's Northern Quarter regeneration project.

Once the central trading area of Victorian Manchester, and the city's main shopping district in the post-war years, it was left under-used and unloved by the retail boom of the sixties and seventies. Now it is undergoing a rebirth, riding high on a tide of urban regeneration.

From mills to thrills

It was once a monument to the city's mighty industrial power. But the days when east Manchester was the "workshop of the world" are long gone, and the Stuart Street power station with them.

Gone too are the grimy mill buildings and smoky towers alongside the banks of the Ashton Canal in Bradford which feature in our archive image.

Thousands of local people were once employed in industry, working for firms like English Steel, the Bradford Gas Works, and the Bradford pit which kept the power station supplied with coal. But millions of pounds have been spent on transforming what subsequently became one of the

city's poorest areas, and our present day scene shows the £110m City of Manchester stadium on the right of the picture.

The Ashton Canal, which runs for almost seven miles between Manchester and Ashton, was built by local business interests in the wake of the success of the Duke of Bridgewater's canal, and the original scheme was completed in 1796. It prospered during the first half of the 19th century, carrying coal to the mills, bringing in raw

materials, taking out manufactured products, and even carrying passengers.

But from the 1930s onwards its fortunes were reversed as smaller mines closed, and the once mighty textile industry also went into decline. In recent times millions of pounds have been spent on restoring the Rochdale and Ashton canals for leisure use.

Different side to a bustling patch

Moss Side is many things to many people but few know it has been home to prime ministers and philosophers.

Manchester's most famous inner suburb started as marshy fields, then filled up with overflow housing for poor Irish and Welsh arrivals during the mid-19th century.

Former prime minister Lloyd George was born in Moss Side in 1863 and renowned German thinker Frederick Engels rented rooms here for his secret Irish girlfriend, Mary Burns. In the 20th century the area became home to a thriving immigrant community.

Alexandra Road in Moss Side in 1960, before all the terraces and local shops were demolished. The photographer is looking towards Moss Lane and the city centre.

Loreto College, which is near St Mary's Church, was the workplace of Oscar-nominated actor Pete Postlethwaite who taught at the convent in the 1960s before entering drama school. Alexandra Road was an important shopping street for residents and was popular with the West Indian community, who also established their own night-time strip of clubs, restaurants, cafes and houses.

The vibrancy and bustle of the area disappeared when, in the 1960s and 1970s, the district was flattened for tower blocks. These days this stretch of Alexandra Road has virtually no shops or cafes and the only landmark remaining is St Mary's Church, which has the tallest spire in Manchester.

free internet access . family history . talking books .
business information . talks . art . homework centres .
language courses . theatre . help for inventors . DVDs .
free events for kids . festivals . silver surfer clubs . local
images collection . bestsellers . author visits . CDs . free
computing courses . newspapers . mobiles . community
information . brilliant books . displays . on-line learning .
reading groups . CD-ROMs . culture . local history . books
for babies . exhibitions . advice . workshops . live poetry .
sheet music . what's on . treasures . coffee . videos .
storytimes . fun

When did you last visit *your* library?

www.manchester.gov.uk/libraries

manchester library
& information service

MANCHESTER
CITY COUNCIL